WHAT IS ARTIFICIAL INTELLIGENCE?

ATHEENA MILAGI PANDIAN S

I ask the indulgence of the biomedical youngsters and beginners who may read this book for dedicating it to a grown-up. I have a serious reason: they are the best engineers I have in the world. I have another reason: this grown-up understands everything, even books about biomedical engineering. I have a third reason: they live in a healthcare world where they are hungry for troubleshooting the medical equipment. They need cheering up. If all these reasons are not enough, I will dedicate the book to the biomedical engineers from whom this grown-up grew. All grown-ups were once biomedical engineers—although few of them remember it. And so I correct my dedication o Biomedical Beginners in the world

Contents

Foreword — vii

Preface — ix

Acknowledgements — xi

Prologue — xiii

1. Introduction On Ai — 1

2. Basics Of Ai — 4

3. Typrs Of Ai — 8

4. Application Of Ai — 11

5. The Evolution Of Ai — 13

Foreword

He is Atheena Milagi Pandian shortly Atheena Pandian from a traditional country India. He has been working hard to build his personal brand over the past 10 years. He was really interested in biomedical sciences especially in medical equipment calibrations, Biomedical updates, and Biomedical related fantasy literature. Medical equipment first appeared in his life when he was at the age of seven. Then he had got his first medical equipment as Stethoscope. He always remembers himself thinking about it was the best thing in the world. He was often playing it whenever he could. but some time later, he really noticed that he could do a lot more things with his medical equipment, During his teenage, he has passion towards on Biomedical Engineering and he plans to design some biomedical projects and research. Due to this impacts, he got under graduation and post-graduation degree in Biomedical Engineering from one of India's top university named as Anna university located in Chennai, then he felt to learn more in hospital management so he did his Master of Business administration in Hospital management and currently he is in the profession to create some quality biomedical engineer to the world.

By

Mr. A.S. ARUMUGA SAKTHI

Mrs. A. PATHMAVATHI

Master. A. SIVAKARTHIKEYAN

Preface

This is my pleasure to give this manuscript to all my Biomedical students those who have a passion towards on the healthcare field, each and every day of life has some disabilities while doing some work or function, that unexpected disabilities maybe affect you physically or mentally but whatever it may be, the self-motivation is the best way to attack anything or any kind of unexpected disabilities in the life. My kind suggestion to the biomedical students is to learn many good things in life and try to clear the disabilities of others.

Acknowledgements

I would like to express my special thanks of gratitude to my father Mr P.A. Shanmuga Nathan as well as my mother Mrs S.Saradhashanmuganathan who gave me the golden opportunity to do this wonderful profession and this profession make me to write a book on this topic which also helped me in doing a lot of manuscript and i came to know about so many new things I am really thankful to them.
Secondly i would also like to thank my wife Mrs A,Sahaya Rooba and my son Master A.Aadhina Vignshwara Pandiyan who helped me a lot in finalizing this book within the limited time frame.

Prologue

Your limitation—it's only your imagination.
    Push yourself, because no one else is going to do it for you.
    Sometimes later becomes never. ...
    Great things never come from comfort zones.
    Dream it. ...
    Success doesn't just find you. ...
    The harder you work for something, the greater you'll feel when you achieve it.
    Dream bigger.

CHAPTER ONE

Introduction on AI

To be franker there are too many definitions some common of them are as follows.

- The ability of a digital computer or computer-controlled robot to perform tasks commonly associated with intelligent beings.

or

- A machine completing the tasks which involve a certain degree of intelligence which was previously deemed only to be done by humans

or

- It is the simulation of human intelligence processes by machines, especially computer systems. These processes include learning, reasoning, and self-correction

or

- The capability of a machine to imitate intelligent human behavior

Introduction

- Artificial intelligence (AI), sometimes called machine intelligence, is intelligence demonstrated by machines, in contrast to the natural intelligence displayed by humans
- Leading AI textbooks define the field as the study of "intelligent agents": any device that perceives its environment and takes actions that maximize its chance of successfully achieving its goals
- Colloquially, the term "artificial intelligence" is often used to describe machines (or computers) that mimic "cognitive" functions that humans associate with the human mind, such as "learning" and "problem solving"
- As machines become increasingly capable, tasks considered to require "intelligence" are often removed from the definition of AI, a phenomenon known as the AI effect.

or

- Artificial Intelligence is an approach to make a computer, a robot, or a product to think about how smart humans think
- AI is a study of how the human brain thinks, learns, decide and work when it tries to solve problems
- And finally, this study outputs intelligent software systems
- The aim of AI is to improve computer functions which are related to human knowledge, for example, reasoning, learning, and problem-solving

- The intelligence is intangible. It is composed of

1. Reasoning
2. Learning
3. Problem Solving
4. Perception
5. Linguistic Intelligence

- The objectives of AI research are reasoning, knowledge representation, planning, learning, natural language processing, realization, and the ability to move and manipulate objects. There are long-term goals in the general intelligence sector
- Approaches include statistical methods, computational intelligence, and traditional coding AI. During the AI research related to search and mathematical optimization, artificial neural networks and methods based on statistics, probability, and economics, we use many tools. Computer science attracts AI in the field of science, mathematics, psychology, linguistics, philosophy and so on.

Need for Artificial Intelligence

- To create expert systems that exhibit intelligent behavior with the capability to learn, demonstrate, explain and advise its users
- Helping machines find solutions to complex problems like humans do and applying them as algorithms in a computer-friendly manner
- Applications of AI include Natural Language Processing, Gaming, Speech Recognition, Vision Systems, Healthcare, Automotive etc
- An AI system is composed of an agent and its environment
- An agent(e.g., human or robot) is anything that can perceive its environment through sensors and acts upon that environment through effectors
- Intelligent agents must be able to set goals and achieve them. In classical planning problems, the agent can assume that it is the only system acting in the world, allowing the agent to be certain of the consequences of its actions
- However, if the agent is not the only actor, then it requires that the agent can reason under uncertainty
- This calls for an agent that cannot only assess its environment and make predictions but also evaluate its predictions and adapt based on its assessment
- Natural language processing gives machines the ability to read and understand human language. Some straightforward applications of natural language processing include information retrieval, text mining, question answering, and machine translation
- Machine perception is the ability to use input from sensors (such as cameras, microphones, sensors, etc.) to deduce aspects of the world. e.g., Computer Vision
- Concepts such as game theory, decision theory, necessitate that an agent is able to detect and model human emotions.
- Many times, students get confused between Machine Learning and Artificial Intelligence, but Machine learning, a fundamental concept of AI research since the field's inception, is the study of computer algorithms that improve automatically through experience
- The mathematical analysis of machine learning algorithms and their performance is a branch of theoretical computer science known as a computational learning theory.
- Scientist divides AI research into three approaches, which he calls computational psychology, computational philosophy, and computer science
- Computational psychology is used to make computer programs that mimic human behavior.

- Computational philosophy is used to develop an adaptive, free-flowing computer mind. Implementing computer science serves the goal of creating computers that can perform tasks that only people could previously accomplish.

AI has developed a large number of tools to solve the most difficult problems in computer science, like:

1. Search and optimization
2. Logic
3. Probabilistic methods for uncertain reasoning
4. Classifiers and statistical learning methods
5. Neural networks
6. Control theory
7. Languages

- High-profile examples of AI include autonomous vehicles (such as drones and self-driving cars), medical diagnosis, creating art (such as poetry), proving mathematical theorems, playing games (such as Chess or Go), search engines (such as Google search), online assistants (such as Siri), image recognition in photographs, spam filtering, prediction of judicial decisions and targeting online advertisements. Other applications include

1. Healthcare, Automotive
2. Finance, Video games, etc

CHAPTER TWO

Basics of AI

When you think of Artificial Intelligence, your thought immediately goes to robots or anything automated. Even though you're right, what if I told you Artificial Intelligence is so much more than just robots.

- Take a look at the image to the left. You could probably tell what they are
- The top one is Google Assistant, found in Google's Pixel Phone line and the bottom is Siri, Apple's friendly assistant found on virtually every Apple device. Both of these virtual assistants are examples of Artificial Intelligence
- Think of it this way, robots are like shells and the computer is the actual AI. It's like the human body. Your brain controls your movements exactly to your specifications
- This is the same concept used in AI
- The computer resembles the brain and it controls all of the movements the robot or machine makes
- AI can manifest itself in many different ways, to name a few we could have machines in an assembly line, all programmed to do a specific task, we could have robot vacuums that vacuum our house whenever we want or we could even have AI taking customers' orders at restaurants.
- These tasks are made to make human life easier. So, the question arises, what is Artificial Intelligence?
- Artificial Intelligence is an umbrella term, covering two main subtopics, Machine Learning, and Deep Learning. Artificial Intelligence was designed so, you don't realize that a machine is doing the job, exactly how a human would.
- AI is basically a broad area of computer science, that allows machines to complete similar tasks to humans
- For example, AI could easily be used when programming an autonomous vehicle
- You could program it to stop at red lights, proceed with caution when passing someone biking or even program it to be able to sense pedestrians jaywalking but, the point of AI is to exhibit human actions. So, if there is someone jaywalking, you could teach the computer to exhibit road rage, like honking the horn and yelling at the jaywalker to move out of the way
- Many of you may not know this but, Artificial Intelligence is not a new concept. It was actually coined in 1956 by Dartmouth Professor, John McCarthy
- As a child, McCarthy was fascinated with any mechanical machine out there, like automobiles or planes. His curiosity sparked when he wanted to know if the machines could learn exactly as children do. He used trial and error to develop formal reasoning, which is how you can determine weak and strong AI
- John McCarthy's theory was proven when computer scientists realized they could actually, teach the AI form (robots, computers, etc.) to do what they needed. It's how we learn as well. We learn by reading and scanning textbooks while, the computer learns the same way, by reading and scanning the internet. All of this learning is done by Machine Learning.

Machine Learning (ML)

- Machine Learning is a type of AI that teaches the machine to act on its own. Similar to humans, machines can retain information and get smarter over time. However, unlike humans, machines aren't susceptible to things like

short-term memory loss, information overload, fatigue or distractions
- After learning all this you may be wondering, how do these machines actually learn? The machines scan through billions of photos a minute to be able to identify anything you want it to. You just need to program what specifics the machine needs to look for
- If I wanted to teach my machine to identify, a cat or a dog. I would want to make sure that the properties of those animals are what the computer looks for when diagnosing the animal.
- I could tell the computer to look for specific things about the appearance of the animal-like:

1. A cat has very prominent and noticeable whiskers while a dog normally doesn't
2. A dog has a short tail, while a cat's tail is very long
3. While standing, cats' legs are close together while dogs' legs are further apart

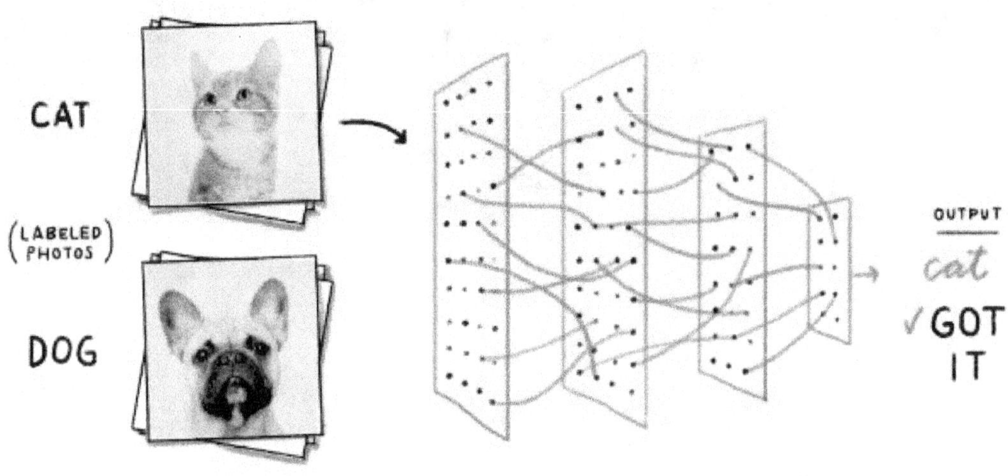

Concept of ML

- They analyze all this information using something called neural networks. Neural networks are basically like a filter for the AI to process and analyze all the information they were looking for. They are able to filter out write and wrong information using linear algebra.

Weak AI

- Like humans, Artificial Intelligence learns the way we do. We are given a textbook or a website, and we retain the information we've read. AI does the same thing, but in a more efficient way, as it has the whole Internet at its disposal
- Fun Fact: Did you know that 90% of the world's data, was created in the past two years! That's crazy!
- In simple terms, weak AI is Artificial Intelligence created to do work on a specific task. It has a limited or "weak" amount of knowledge
- For example, assume the robot to the below was programmed to only tell me what the weather is. If I ask it what is the weather, it would be able to tell me, "three degrees celsius, with a high of seven degrees celsius".

Robot

- This is because all of its information is coming from one source. However, if I ask it to tell me the time in San Francisco, it's going to get confused and not be able to answer my question. This is because I haven't programmed it to analyze a world clock.
- Weak AI is simulating thinking and does not have the ability to think or make decisions on its own.

Strong AI

- Machine Learning is the key component in developing strong AI. Essentially, the AI form has mental abilities and functions that mimic the human brain. In the philosophy of strong AI, there is no difference between the form of AI exactly imitating the actions of the human brain, and the actions of a human being. Developing its power of understanding and its consciousness are still trying to be developed and implemented
- Google created an AI bot of their own. This bot is considered strong AI. It has the ability to come to conclusions about itself and is aware of its presence on earth. Google's Artificial Intelligence Bot even stated that "the purpose of living is to live forever". This shows that the bot is even aware that it doesn't possess human parts, and is, therefore, "immortal"
- Fun fact: John Searle, the American philosopher that coined the term strong and weak AI, agrees with the notion that machines can have such consciousness and understanding because he wrote, "we (as in humans) are able to be such machines as our minds can mimic the behavior that any strong AI can." He is one of the only philosophers who believe in this AI phenomenon
- The concept of strong AI is very philosophical, as humans can't define what intelligence really is. It is very difficult to give clear criteria as to what would count as a success in the development of strong AI. This is because it is a different perception of AI, which makes AI equal to the human mind. It stipulates that a computer

can be programmed to actually be a human mind, to have beliefs, perceptions and other cognitive states that are traditional, ascribed to humans

- An example of strong AI is IBM's Watson. A supercomputer that has been taught, literally, everything. In the photo above, it is playing Jeopardy with the two smartest players to be featured on that show, Ken Jennings and Brad Rutter. Watson clearly won because of his ability to scan the internet at rapid speeds (to be able to correctly respond)
- The way I see it, strong AI will be the future of this society. As time goes on, I believe that humans will be able to answer all the questions we have about philosophy and life.
-

CHAPTER THREE

Typrs of AI

AI can be classified in any number of ways there are two types of main classification.

Type1:

- **Weak AI or Narrow AI:** It is focused on one narrow task, the phenomenon that machines which are not too intelligent to do their own work can be built in such a way that they seem smart. An example would be a poker game where a machine beats humans where in which all rules and moves are fed into the machine. Here each and every possible scenario needs to be entered beforehand manually. Each and every weak AI will contribute to the building of strong AI
- **Strong AI:** The machines that can actually think and perform tasks on its own just like a human being. There are no proper existing examples for this but some industry leaders are very keen on getting close to build a strong AI which has resulted in rapid progress.

Type2(based on functionalities):

- **Reactive Machines:** This is one of the basic forms of AI. It doesn't have past memory and cannot use past information to information for the future actions. Example:- IBM chess program that beat Garry Kasparov in the 1990s
- **Limited Memory:** AI systems can use past experiences to inform future decisions. Some of the decision-making functions in self-driving cars have been designed this way. Observations used to inform actions happening in the not so distant future, such as a car that has changed lanes. These observations are not stored permanently and also Apple's Chatbot Siri
- **Theory of Mind:** This type of AI should be able to understand people's emotion, belief, thoughts, expectations and be able to interact socially Even though a lot of improvements are there in this field this kind of AI is not complete yet
- **Self-awareness:** An AI that has it's own conscious, super-intelligent, self-awareness and sentient (In simple words a complete human being). Of course, this kind of bot also doesn't exist and if achieved it will be one of the milestones in the field of AI.

There are many ways AI can be achieved some of them are as follows:

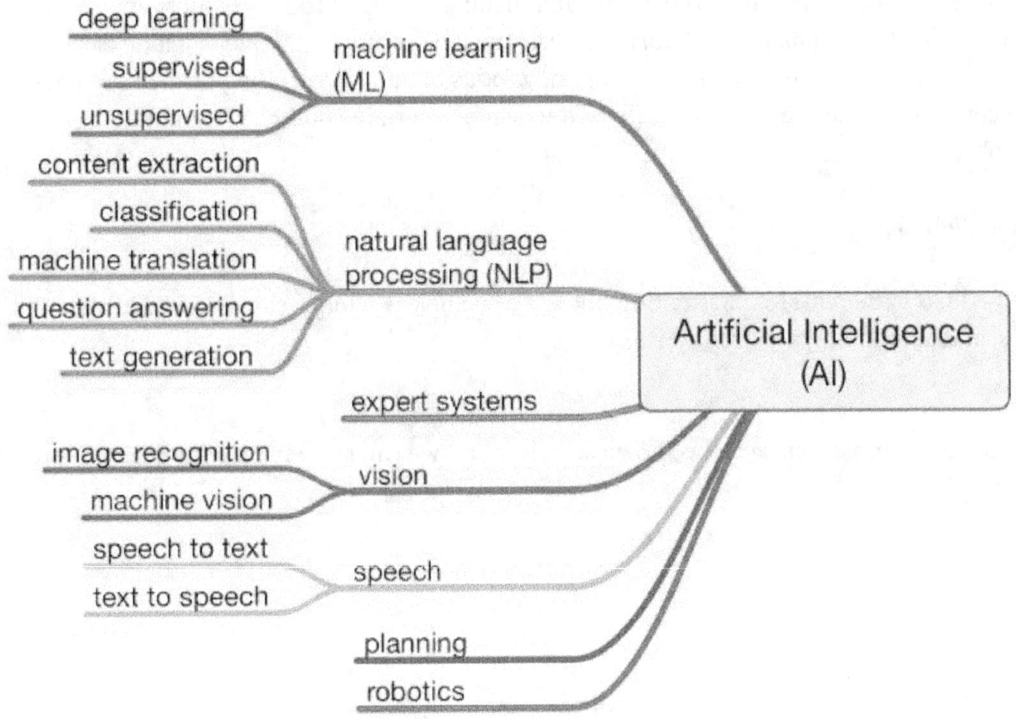

Many ways AI can be achieved

The most important among them are as follows:
Machine Learning (ML)

- It is a method where the target(goal) is defined and the steps to reach that target is learned by the machine itself by training(gaining experience).For example to identify a simple object such as an apple or orange. The target is achieved not by explicitly specifying the details about it and coding it but it is just as we teach a child by showing multiple different pictures of it and therefore allowing the machine to define the steps to identify it like an apple or an orange.

Natural Language Processing (NLP)

- Natural Language Processing is broadly defined as the automatic manipulation of natural language, like speech and text, by software. One of the well-known examples of this is email spam detection as we can see how it has improved in our mail system.

Vision

- It can be said as a field that enables the machines to see. Machine vision captures and analyses visual information using a camera, analog-to-digital conversion, and digital signal processing. It can be compared to human eyesight but it is not bound by the human limitation which can enable it to see through walls(now that would be interesting if we can have implants that can make us see through the wall). It is usually achieved through machine learning to get the best possible results so we could say that these two fields are interlinked.

Robotics

- It is a field of engineering focused on the design and manufacturing of robots. Robots are often used to perform tasks that are difficult for humans to perform or perform consistently. Examples include car assembly lines, in hospitals, office cleaner, serving foods, and preparing foods in hotels, patrolling farm areas and even as police officers. Recently machine learning has been used to achieve certain good results in building robots that interact socially(Sophia)

Autonomous Vehicles

- This area of AI has gathered a lot of attention. the list of vehicles includes cars, buses, trucks, trains, ships, submarines, and autopilot flying drones, etc.

The fields above in simple terms can be shown as below and we can see why machine learning plays a major role in achieving AI

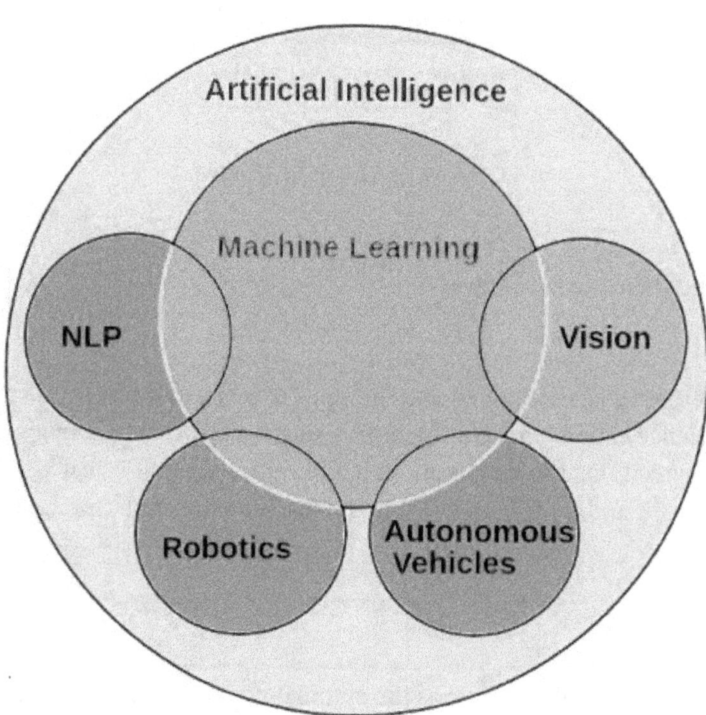

Fields of AI

CHAPTER FOUR

Application of AI

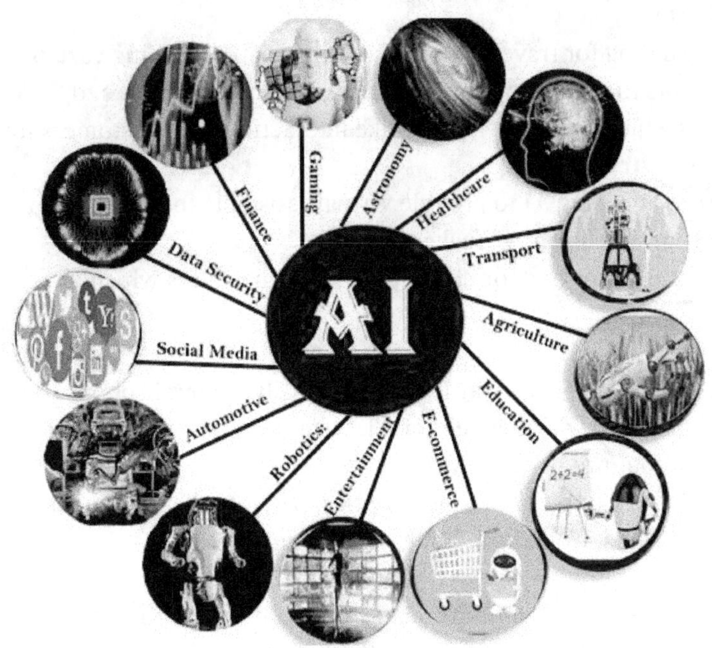

Applications of AI

Artificial Intelligence has various applications in today's society. It is becoming essential for today's time because it can solve complex problems in an efficient way in multiple industries, such as Healthcare, entertainment, finance, education, etc. AI is making our daily life more comfortable and fast.

Following are some sectors which have the application of Artificial Intelligence:

1. AI in Astronomy

Artificial Intelligence can be very useful to solve complex universe problems. AI technology can be helpful for understanding the universe such as how it works, origin, etc.

2. AI in Healthcare

In the last, five to ten years, AI becoming more advantageous for the healthcare industry and going to have a significant impact on this industry.

Healthcare Industries are applying AI to make a better and faster diagnosis than humans. AI can help doctors with diagnoses and can inform when patients are worsening so that medical help can reach to the patient before hospitalization.

3. AI in Gaming

AI can be used for gaming purposes. The AI machines can play strategic games like chess, where the machine needs to think of a large number of possible places.

4. AI in Finance

AI and finance industries are the best matches for each other. The finance industry is implementing automation, chatbot, adaptive intelligence, algorithm trading, and machine learning into financial processes.

5. AI in Data Security

The security of data is crucial for every company and cyber-attacks are growing very rapidly in the digital world. AI can be used to make your data more safe and secure. Some examples such as AEG bot, AI2 Platform, are used to determine software bug and cyber-attacks in a better way.

6. AI in Social Media

Social Media sites such as Facebook, Twitter, and Snapchat contain billions of user profiles, which need to be stored and managed in a very efficient way. AI can organize and manage massive amounts of data. AI can analyze lots of data to identify the latest trends, hashtags, and requirements of different users.

7. AI in Travel & Transport

AI is becoming highly demanding for travel industries. AI is capable of doing various travel related works such as from making travel arrangements to suggesting the hotels, flights, and best routes to the customers. Travel industries are using AI-powered chatbots which can make human-like interaction with customers for a better and fast response.

8. AI in the Automotive Industry

Some Automotive industries are using AI to provide virtual assistants to their use for better performance. Such as Tesla has introduced TeslaBot, an intelligent virtual assistant.

Various Industries are currently working for developing self-driven cars which can make your journey more safe and secure.

9. AI in Robotics:

Artificial Intelligence has a remarkable role in Robotics. Usually, general robots are programmed such that they can perform some repetitive task, but with the help of AI, we can create intelligent robots which can perform tasks with their own experiences without pre-programmed.

Humanoid Robots are the best examples for AI in robotics, recently the intelligent Humanoid robot named Erica and Sophia has been developed which can talk and behave like humans.

10. AI in Entertainment

We are currently using some AI-based applications in our daily life with some entertainment services such as Netflix or Amazon. With the help of ML/AI algorithms, these services show the recommendations for programs or shows.

11. AI in Agriculture

Agriculture is an area that requires various resources, labor, money, and time for best result. Now a day's agriculture is becoming digital, and AI is emerging in this field. Agriculture is applying AI as agriculture robotics, solid and crop monitoring, predictive analysis. AI in agriculture can be very helpful for farmers.

12. AI in E-commerce

AI is providing a competitive edge to the e-commerce industry, and it is becoming more demanding in the e-commerce business. AI is helping shoppers to discover associated products with recommended size, color, or even brand.

13. AI in education:

AI can automate grading so that the tutor can have more time to teach. AI chatbot can communicate with students as a teaching assistant.

AI in the future can be work as a personal virtual tutor for students, which will be accessible easily at any time and any place.

CHAPTER FIVE

The Evolution of AI

There's virtually no major industry modern AI — more specifically, "narrow AI," which performs objective functions using data-trained models and often falls into the categories of deep learning or machine learning — hasn't already affected. That's especially true in the past few years, as data collection and analysis has ramped up considerably thanks to robust IoT connectivity, the proliferation of connected devices and ever-speedier computer processing.

Some sectors are at the start of their AI journey, others are veteran travelers. Both have a long way to go. Regardless, the impact artificial intelligence is having on our present-day lives is hard to ignore:

Transportation: Although it could take a decade or more to perfect them, autonomous cars will one day ferry us from place to place.

Manufacturing: AI-powered robots work alongside humans to perform a limited range of tasks like assembly and stacking, and predictive analysis sensors keep equipment running smoothly.

Healthcare: In the comparatively AI-nascent field of healthcare, diseases are more quickly and accurately diagnosed, drug discovery is sped up and streamlined, virtual nursing assistants monitor patients and big data analysis helps to create a more personalized patient experience.

Education: Textbooks are digitized with the help of AI, early-stage virtual tutors assist human instructors and facial analysis gauges the emotions of students to help determine who's struggling or bored and better tailor the experience to their individual needs.

Media: Journalism is harnessing AI, too, and will continue to benefit from it. Bloomberg uses Cyborg technology to help make a quick sense of complex financial reports. The Associated Press employs the natural language abilities of Automated Insights to produce 3,700 earning reports stories per year — nearly four times more than in the recent past.

Customer Service: Last but hardly least, Google is working on an AI assistant that can place human-like calls to make appointments at, say, your neighborhood hair salon. In addition to words, the system understands context and nuance

But those advances (and numerous others, including this crop of new ones) are only the beginning; there's much more to come — more than anyone, even the most prescient prognosticators, can fathom.

Most researchers agree that a superintelligent AI is unlikely to exhibit human emotions like love or hate, and that there is no reason to expect AI to become intentionally benevolent or malevolent. Instead, when considering how AI might become a risk, experts think two scenarios most likely:

The AI is programmed to do something devastating: Autonomous weapons are artificial intelligence systems that are programmed to kill. In the hands of the wrong person, these weapons could easily cause mass casualties. Moreover, an AI arms race could inadvertently lead to an AI war that also results in mass casualties. To avoid being thwarted by the enemy, these weapons would be designed to be extremely difficult to simply "turn off," so humans could plausibly lose control of such a situation. This risk is one that's present even with narrow AI but grows as levels of AI intelligence and autonomy increase.

The AI is programmed to do something beneficial, but it develops a destructive method for achieving its goal: This can happen whenever we fail to fully align the AI's goals with ours, which is strikingly difficult. If you ask an obedient intelligent car to take you to the airport as fast as possible, it might get you there chased by helicopters and covered in vomit, doing not what you wanted but literally what you asked for. If a superintelligent system is tasked with an ambitious geoengineering project, it might wreak havoc with our ecosystem as a side effect, and view human attempts to stop it as a threat to be met.

As these examples illustrate, the concern about advanced AI isn't malevolence but competence. A super-intelligent AI will be extremely good at accomplishing its goals, and if those goals aren't aligned with ours, we have a problem. You're probably not an evil ant-hater who steps on ants out of malice, but if you're in charge of a hydroelectric green energy project and there's an anthill in the region to be flooded, too bad for the ants. A key goal of AI safety research is to never place humanity in the position of those ants.

WHY THE RECENT INTEREST IN AI SAFETY

Stephen Hawking, Elon Musk, Steve Wozniak, Bill Gates, and many other big names in science and technology have recently expressed concern in the media and via open letters about the risks posed by AI, joined by many leading AI researchers. Why is the subject suddenly in the headlines?

The idea that the quest for strong AI would ultimately succeed was long thought of as science fiction, centuries or more away. However, thanks to recent breakthroughs, many AI milestones, which experts viewed as decades away merely five years ago, have now been reached, making many experts take seriously the possibility of superintelligence in our lifetime. While some experts still guess that human-level AI is centuries away, most AI researches at the 2015 Puerto Rico Conference guessed that it would happen before 2060. Since it may take decades to complete the required safety research, it is prudent to start it now.

Because AI has the potential to become more intelligent than any human, we have no surefire way of predicting how it will behave. We can't use past technological developments as much of a basis because we've never created anything that has the ability to, wittingly or unwittingly, outsmart us. The best example of what we could face may be our own evolution. People now control the planet, not because we're the strongest, fastest or biggest, but because we're the smartest. If we're no longer the smartest, are we assured to remain in control?

FLI's position is that our civilization will flourish as long as we win the race between the growing power of technology and the wisdom with which we manage it. In the case of AI technology, FLI's position is that the best way to win that race is not to impede the former but to accelerate the latter, by supporting AI safety research.

THE TOP MYTHS ABOUT ADVANCED AI

A captivating conversation is taking place about the future of artificial intelligence and what it will/should mean for humanity. There are fascinating controversies where the world's leading experts disagree, such as: AI's future impact on the job market; if/when human-level AI will be developed; whether this will lead to an intelligence explosion; and whether this is something we should welcome or fear. But there are also many examples of boring pseudo-controversies caused by people misunderstanding and talking past each other. To help ourselves focus on the interesting controversies and open questions — and not on the misunderstandings — let's clear up some of the most common myths.

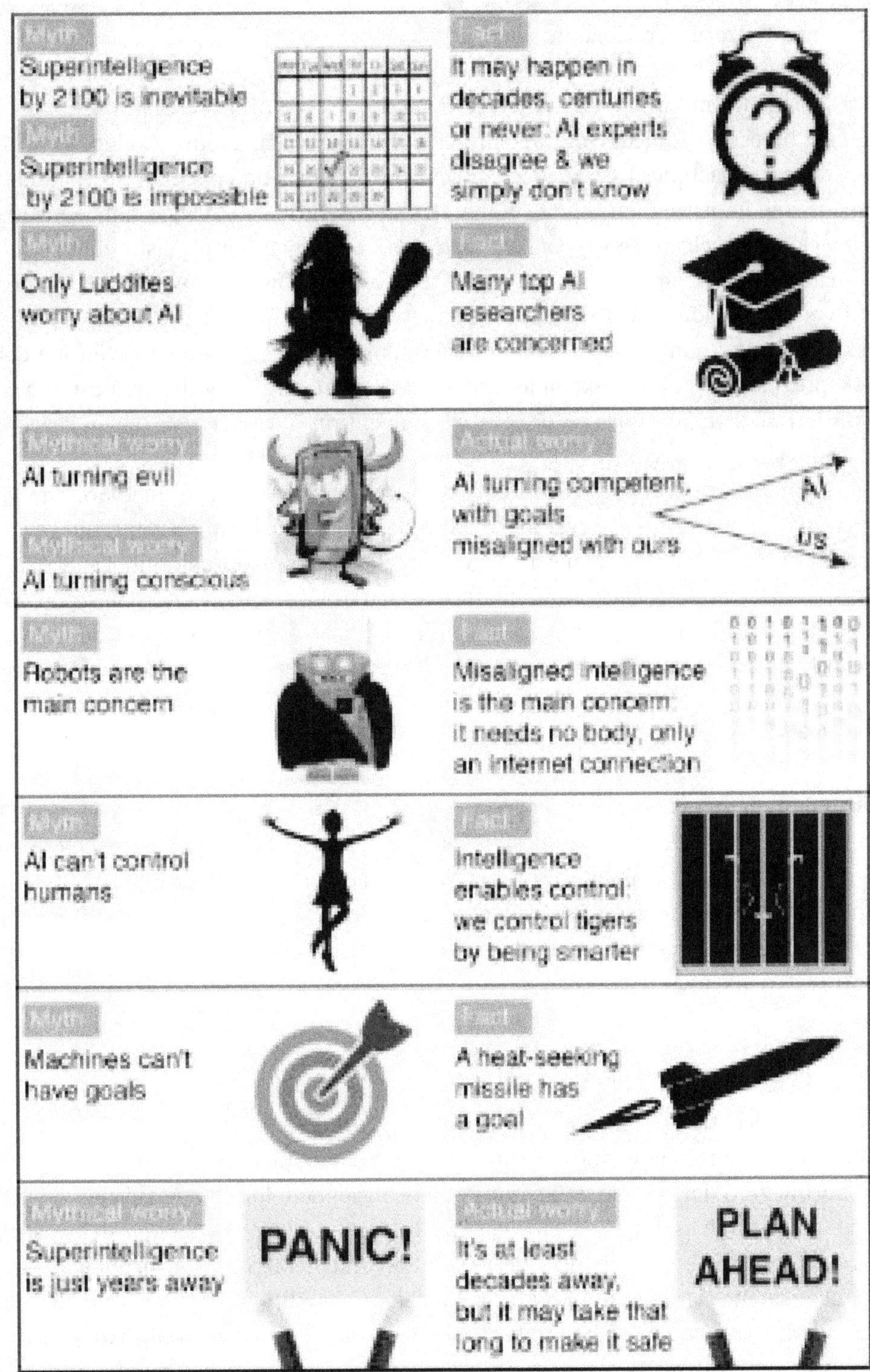

TIMELINE MYTHS

- The first myth regards the timeline: how long will it take until machines greatly supersede human-level intelligence? A common misconception is that we know the answer with great certainty

- One popular myth is that we know we'll get superhuman AI this century. In fact, history is full of technological over-hyping. Where are those fusion power plants and flying cars we were promised we'd have by now? AI has also been repeatedly over-hyped in the past, even by some of the founders of the field. For example, John McCarthy (who coined the term "artificial intelligence")

- Marvin Minsky, Nathaniel Rochester, and Claude Shannon wrote this overly optimistic forecast about what could be accomplished during two months with stone-age computers: "We propose that a 2 month, 10 man study of artificial intelligence be carried out during the summer of 1956 at Dartmouth College [...] An attempt will be made to find how to make machines use language, form abstractions, and concepts, solve kinds of problems now reserved for humans, and improve themselves. We think that a significant advance can be made in one or more of these problems if a carefully selected group of scientists work on it together for a summer."

- On the other hand, a popular counter-myth is that we know we won't get superhuman AI this century. Researchers have made a wide range of estimates for how far we are from superhuman AI, but we certainly can't say with great confidence that the probability is zero this century, given the dismal track record of such techno-skeptic predictions. For example, Ernest Rutherford, arguably the greatest nuclear physicist of his time, said in 1933 — less than 24 hours before Szilard's invention of the nuclear chain reaction — that nuclear energy was "moonshine."

- And Astronomer Royal Richard Woolley called interplanetary travel "utter bilge" in 1956. The most extreme form of this myth is that superhuman AI will never arrive because it's physically impossible. However, physicists know that a brain consists of quarks and electrons arranged to act as a powerful computer and that there's no law of physics preventing us from building even more intelligent quark blobs.

- There have been a number of surveys asking AI researchers how many years from now they think we'll have human-level AI with at least 50% probability. All these surveys have the same conclusion: the world's leading experts disagree, so we simply don't know. For example, in such a poll of the AI researchers at the 2015 Puerto Rico AI conference, the average (median) answer was by year 2045, but some researchers guessed hundreds of years or more.

- There's also a related myth that people who worry about AI think it's only a few years away. In fact, most people on record worrying about superhuman AI guess it's still at least decades away. But they argue that as long as we're not 100% sure that it won't happen this century, it's smart to start safety research now to prepare for the eventuality. Many of the safety problems associated with human-level AI are so hard that they may take decades to solve. So it's prudent to start researching them now rather than the night before some programmers drinking Red Bull decide to switch one on.

CONTROVERSY MYTHS

- Another common misconception is that the only people harboring concerns about AI and advocating AI safety research are Luddites who don't know much about AI. When Stuart Russell, author of the standard AI textbook, mentioned this during his Puerto Rico talk, the audience laughed loudly. A related misconception is that supporting AI safety research is hugely controversial. In fact, to support a modest investment in AI safety research, people don't need to be convinced that risks are high, merely non-negligible — just as a modest investment in home insurance is justified by a non-negligible probability of the home burning down.

- It may be that the media have made the AI safety debate seem more controversial than it really is. After all, fear sells, and articles using out-of-context quotes to proclaim imminent doom can generate more clicks than nuanced and balanced ones. As a result, two people who only know about each other's positions from media quotes are likely to think they disagree more than they really do. For example, a techno-skeptic who only read about Bill Gates's position in a British tabloid may mistakenly think Gates believes superintelligence to be imminent. Similarly, someone in the beneficial-AI movement who knows nothing about Andrew Ng's position except his quote about overpopulation on Mars may mistakenly think he doesn't care about AI safety, whereas in fact, he does. The crux is simply that because Ng's timeline estimates are longer, he naturally tends to prioritize short-term AI challenges over long-term ones.

MYTHS ABOUT THE RISKS OF SUPERHUMAN AI

- Many AI researchers roll their eyes when seeing this headline: "Stephen Hawking warns that rise of robots may be disastrous for mankind." And as many have lost count of how many similar articles they've seen. Typically, these articles are accompanied by an evil-looking robot carrying a weapon, and they suggest we should worry about robots rising up and killing us because they've become conscious and/or evil. On a lighter note, such articles are actually rather impressive, because they succinctly summarize the scenario that AI researchers don't worry about. That scenario combines as many as three separate misconceptions: concern about consciousness, evil, and robots.
- If you drive down the road, you have a subjective experience of colors, sounds, etc. But does a self-driving car have a subjective experience? Does it feel like anything at all to be a self-driving car? Although this mystery of consciousness is interesting in its own right, it's irrelevant to AI risk. If you get struck by a driverless car, it makes no difference to you whether it subjectively feels conscious. In the same way, what will affect us humans is what superintelligent AI does, not how it subjectively feels.
- The fear of machines turning evil is another red herring. The real worry isn't malevolence, but competence. A superintelligent AI is by definition very good at attaining its goals, whatever they may be, so we need to ensure that its goals are aligned with ours. Humans don't generally hate ants, but we're more intelligent than they are – so if we want to build a hydroelectric dam and there's an anthill there, too bad for the ants. The beneficial-AI movement wants to avoid placing humanity in the position of those ants.
- Consciousness misconception is related to the myth that machines can't have goals. Machines can obviously have goals in the narrow sense of exhibiting goal-oriented behavior: the behavior of a heat-seeking missile is most economically explained as a goal to hit a target. If you feel threatened by a machine whose goals are misaligned with yours, then it is precisely its goals in this narrow sense that troubles you, not whether the machine is conscious and experiences a sense of purpose. If that heat-seeking missile were chasing you, you probably wouldn't exclaim: "I'm not worried, because machines can't have goals!"
- I sympathize with Rodney Brooks and other robotics pioneers who feel unfairly demonized by scaremongering tabloids because some journalists seem obsessively fixated on robots and adorn many of their articles with evil-looking metal monsters with red shiny eyes. In fact, the main concern of the beneficial-AI movement isn't with robots but with intelligence itself: specifically, intelligence whose goals are misaligned with ours. To cause us trouble, such misaligned superhuman intelligence needs no robotic body, merely an internet connection – this may enable outsmarting financial markets, out-inventing human researchers, out-manipulating human leaders, and developing weapons we cannot even understand. Even if building robots were physically impossible, a super-intelligent and super-wealthy AI could easily pay or manipulate many humans to unwittingly do its bidding.
- The robot misconception is related to the myth that machines can't control humans. Intelligence enables control: humans control tigers not because we are stronger, but because we are smarter. This means that if we cede our position as smartest on our planet, it's possible that we might also cede control.

THE INTERESTING CONTROVERSIES

- Not wasting time on the above-mentioned misconceptions lets us focus on true and interesting controversies where even the experts disagree. What sort of future do you want? Should we develop lethal autonomous weapons? What would you like to happen with job automation? What career advice would you give today's kids? Do you prefer new jobs replacing the old ones or a jobless society where everyone enjoys a life of leisure and machine-produced wealth? Further down the road, would you like us to create superintelligent life and spread it through our cosmos? Will we control intelligent machines or will they control us? Will intelligent machines replace us, coexist with us, or merge with us? What will it mean to be human in the age of artificial intelligence? What would you like it to mean, and how can we make the future be that way? Please join the conversation!